HAL•LEONARD
INSTRUMENTAL
PLAY-ALONG

AUDIO
ACCESS
INCLUDED

PLAYBACK+
Speed • Pitch • Balance • Loop

VIOLA

CLASSIC ROCK

Audio Arrangements by Peter Deneff

To access audio visit:
www.halleonard.com/mylibrary

Enter Code
1636-7944-4347-0124

ISBN 978-1-5400-5332-9

HAL•LEONARD®

Visit Hal Leonard Online at
www.halleonard.com

Contact us:
Hal Leonard
7777 West Bluemound Road
Milwaukee, WI 53213
Email: info@halleonard.com

In Europe, contact:
Hal Leonard Europe Limited
42 Wigmore Street
Marylebone, London, W1U 2RN
Email: info@halleonardeurope.com

In Australia, contact:
Hal Leonard Australia Pty. Ltd.
4 Lentara Court
Cheltenham, Victoria, 3192 Australia
Email: info@halleonard.com.au

DON'T FEAR THE REAPER

VIOLA

Words and Music by
DONALD ROESER

FORTUNATE SON

VIOLA

Words and Music by
JOHN FOGERTY

FREE FALLIN'

VIOLA

Words and Music by TOM PETTY
and JEFF LYNNE

GO YOUR OWN WAY

VIOLA

Words and Music by
LINDSEY BUCKINGHAM

IT'S ONLY ROCK AND ROLL
(But I Like It)

VIOLA

Words and Music by MICK JAGGER
and KEITH RICHARDS

JACK AND DIANE

VIOLA

Words and Music by
JOHN MELLENCAMP

LAYLA

VIOLA

Words and Music by ERIC CLAPTON
and JIM GORDON

THE LOGICAL SONG

VIOLA

Words and Music by RICK DAVIES
and ROGER HODGSON

MONEY

VIOLA

Words and Music by
ROGER WATERS

MORE THAN A FEELING

VIOLA

Words and Music by
TOM SCHOLZ

OLD TIME ROCK & ROLL

VIOLA

Words and Music by GEORGE JACKSON
and THOMAS E. JONES III

MY LIFE

VIOLA

Words and Music by
BILLY JOEL

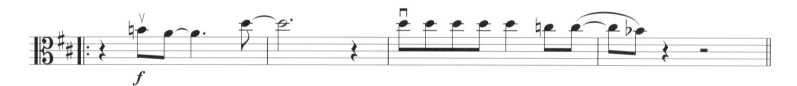

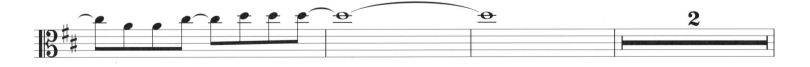

RENEGADE

VIOLA

Words and Music by
TOMMY SHAW

SWEET HOME ALABAMA

VIOLA

Words and Music by RONNIE VAN ZANT,
ED KING and GARY ROSSINGTON

Moderate Country Rock

25 OR 6 TO 4

VIOLA

Words and Music by
ROBERT LAMM

HAL•LEONARD INSTRUMENTAL PLAY-ALONG

Your favorite songs are arranged just for solo instrumentalists with this outstanding series. Each book includes great full-accompaniment play-along audio so you can sound just like a pro! Check out **www.halleonard.com** to see all the titles available.

The Beatles

All You Need Is Love • Blackbird • Day Tripper • Eleanor Rigby • Get Back • Here, There and Everywhere • Hey Jude • I Will • Let It Be • Lucy in the Sky with Diamonds • Ob-La-Di, Ob-La-Da • Penny Lane • Something • Ticket to Ride • Yesterday.

_____	00225330	Flute	$14.99
_____	00225331	Clarinet	$14.99
_____	00225332	Alto Sax	$14.99
_____	00225333	Tenor Sax	$14.99
_____	00225334	Trumpet.	$14.99
_____	00225335	Horn	$14.99
_____	00225336	Trombone	$14.99
_____	00225337	Violin.	$14.99
_____	00225338	Viola	$14.99
_____	00225339	Cello	$14.99

Chart Hits

All About That Bass • All of Me • Happy • Radioactive • Roar • Say Something • Shake It Off • A Sky Full of Stars • Someone like You • Stay with Me • Thinking Out Loud • Uptown Funk.

_____	00146207	Flute	$12.99
_____	00146208	Clarinet	$12.99
_____	00146209	Alto Sax	$12.99
_____	00146210	Tenor Sax	$12.99
_____	00146211	Trumpet.	$12.99
_____	00146212	Horn	$12.99
_____	00146213	Trombone	$12.99
_____	00146214	Violin.	$12.99
_____	00146215	Viola	$12.99
_____	00146216	Cello	$12.99

Disney Greats

Arabian Nights • Hawaiian Roller Coaster Ride • It's a Small World • Look Through My Eyes • Yo Ho (A Pirate's Life for Me) • and more.

_____	00841934	Flute	$12.99
_____	00841935	Clarinet	$12.99
_____	00841936	Alto Sax	$12.99
_____	00841937	Tenor Sax	$12.95
_____	00841938	Trumpet.	$12.99
_____	00841939	Horn	$12.99
_____	00841940	Trombone	$12.99
_____	00841941	Violin.	$12.99
_____	00841942	Viola	$12.99
_____	00841943	Cello	$12.99
_____	00842078	Oboe	$12.99

The Greatest Showman

Come Alive • From Now On • The Greatest Show • A Million Dreams • Never Enough • The Other Side • Rewrite the Stars • This Is Me • Tightrope.

_____	00277389	Flute	$14.99
_____	00277390	Clarinet	$14.99
_____	00277391	Alto Sax	$14.99
_____	00277392	Tenor Sax	$14.99
_____	00277393	Trumpet.	$14.99
_____	00277394	Horn	$14.99
_____	00277395	Trombone	$14.99
_____	00277396	Violin.	$14.99
_____	00277397	Viola	$14.99
_____	00277398	Cello	$14.99

Movie and TV Music

The Avengers • Doctor Who XI • Downton Abbey • Game of Thrones • Guardians of the Galaxy • Hawaii Five-O • Married Life • Rey's Theme (from *Star Wars: The Force Awakens*) • The X-Files • and more.

_____	00261807	Flute	$12.99
_____	00261808	Clarinet	$12.99
_____	00261809	Alto Sax	$12.99
_____	00261810	Tenor Sax	$12.99
_____	00261811	Trumpet.	$12.99
_____	00261812	Horn	$12.99
_____	00261813	Trombone	$12.99
_____	00261814	Violin. and	$12.99
_____	00261815	Viola	$12.99
_____	00261816	Cello	$12.99

12 Pop Hits

Believer • Can't Stop the Feeling • Despacito • It Ain't Me • Look What You Made Me Do • Million Reasons • Perfect • Send My Love (To Your New Lover) • Shape of You • Slow Hands • Too Good at Goodbyes • What About Us.

_____	00261790	Flute	$12.99
_____	00261791	Clarinet	$12.99
_____	00261792	Alto Sax	$12.99
_____	00261793	Tenor Sax	$12.99
_____	00261794	Trumpet.	$12.99
_____	00261795	Horn	$12.99
_____	00261796	Trombone	$12.99
_____	00261797	Violin.	$12.99
_____	00261798	Viola	$12.99
_____	00261799	Cello	$12.99

Songs from Frozen, Tangled and Enchanted

Do You Want to Build a Snowman? • For the First Time in Forever • Happy Working Song • I See the Light • In Summer • Let It Go • Mother Knows Best • That's How You Know • True Love's First Kiss • When Will My Life Begin • and more.

_____	00126921	Flute	$14.99
_____	00126922	Clarinet	$14.99
_____	00126923	Alto Sax	$14.99
_____	00126924	Tenor Sax	$14.99
_____	00126925	Trumpet.	$14.99
_____	00126926	Horn	$14.99
_____	00126927	Trombone	$14.99
_____	00126928	Violin.	$14.99
_____	00126929	Viola	$14.99
_____	00126930	Cello	$14.99

Top Hits

Adventure of a Lifetime • Budapest • Die a Happy Man • Ex's & Oh's • Fight Song • Hello • Let It Go • Love Yourself • One Call Away • Pillowtalk • Stitches • Writing's on the Wall.

_____	00171073	Flute	$12.99
_____	00171074	Clarinet	$12.99
_____	00171075	Alto Sax	$12.99
_____	00171106	Tenor Sax	$12.99
_____	00171107	Trumpet.	$12.99
_____	00171108	Horn	$12.99
_____	00171109	Trombone	$12.99
_____	00171110	Violin.	$12.99
_____	00171111	Viola	$12.99
_____	00171112	Cello	$12.99

Wicked

As Long As You're Mine • Dancing Through Life • Defying Gravity • For Good • I'm Not That Girl • Popular • The Wizard and I • and more.

_____	00842236	Flute	$12.99
_____	00842237	Clarinet	$12.99
_____	00842238	Alto Saxophone	$12.99
_____	00842239	Tenor Saxophone.	$11.95
_____	00842240	Trumpet.	$12.99
_____	00842241	Horn	$12.99
_____	00842242	Trombone	$12.99
_____	00842243	Violin.	$12.99
_____	00842244	Viola	$12.99
_____	00842245	Cello	$12.99

Prices, contents, and availability subject to change without notice.
Disney characters and Artwork ™ & © 2018 Disney

HAL•LEONARD®

101 SONGS

BIG COLLECTIONS OF FAVORITE SONGS ARRANGED FOR SOLO INSTRUMENTALISTS.

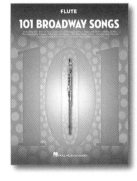

101 BROADWAY SONGS

00154199	Flute	$14.99
00154200	Clarinet	$14.99
00154201	Alto Sax	$14.99
00154202	Tenor Sax	$14.99
00154203	Trumpet	$14.99
00154204	Horn	$14.99
00154205	Trombone	$14.99
00154206	Violin	$14.99
00154207	Viola	$14.99
00154208	Cello	$14.99

101 CHRISTMAS SONGS

00278637	Flute	$14.99
00278638	Clarinet	$14.99
00278639	Alto Sax	$14.99
00278640	Tenor Sax	$14.99
00278641	Trumpet	$14.99
00278642	Horn	$14.99
00278643	Trombone	$14.99
00278644	Violin	$14.99
00278645	Viola	$14.99
00278646	Cello	$14.99

101 CLASSICAL THEMES

00155315	Flute	$14.99
00155317	Clarinet	$14.99
00155318	Alto Sax	$14.99
00155319	Tenor Sax	$14.99
00155320	Trumpet	$14.99
00155321	Horn	$14.99
00155322	Trombone	$14.99
00155323	Violin	$14.99
00155324	Viola	$14.99
00155325	Cello	$14.99

101 DISNEY SONGS

00244104	Flute	$16.99
00244106	Clarinet	$16.99
00244107	Alto Sax	$16.99
00244108	Tenor Sax	$16.99
00244109	Trumpet	$16.99
00244112	Horn	$16.99
00244120	Trombone	$16.99
00244121	Violin	$16.99
00244125	Viola	$16.99
00244126	Cello	$16.99

101 HIT SONGS

00194561	Flute	$16.99
00197182	Clarinet	$16.99
00197183	Alto Sax	$16.99
00197184	Tenor Sax	$16.99
00197185	Trumpet	$16.99
00197186	Horn	$16.99
00197187	Trombone	$16.99
00197188	Violin	$16.99
00197189	Viola	$16.99
00197190	Cello	$16.99

101 JAZZ SONGS

00146363	Flute	$14.99
00146364	Clarinet	$14.99
00146366	Alto Sax	$14.99
00146367	Tenor Sax	$14.99
00146368	Trumpet	$14.99
00146369	Horn	$14.99
00146370	Trombone	$14.99
00146371	Violin	$14.99
00146372	Viola	$14.99
00146373	Cello	$14.99

101 MOVIE HITS

00158087	Flute	$14.99
00158088	Clarinet	$14.99
00158089	Alto Sax	$14.99
00158090	Tenor Sax	$14.99
00158091	Trumpet	$14.99
00158092	Horn	$14.99
00158093	Trombone	$14.99
00158094	Violin	$14.99
00158095	Viola	$14.99
00158096	Cello	$14.99

101 POPULAR SONGS

00224722	Flute	$16.99
00224723	Clarinet	$16.99
00224724	Alto Sax	$16.99
00224725	Tenor Sax	$16.99
00224726	Trumpet	$16.99
00224727	Horn	$16.99
00224728	Trombone	$16.99
00224729	Violin	$16.99
00224730	Viola	$16.99
00224731	Cello	$16.99

HAL•LEONARD®
www.halleonard.com

Prices, contents and availability subject to change without notice.